# A TREE IS FOR...

## Judith Bauer Stamper

**Teaching**Strategies™ • Washington D.C.

For Teaching Strategies, Inc.
Publisher: Larry Bram
Editorial Director: Hilary Parrish Nelson
VP Curriculum and Assessment: Cate Heroman
Product Manager: Kai-leé Berke
Book Development Team: Sherrie Rudick and Jan Greenberg
Project Manager: Jo A. Wilson

For Q2AMedia
Editorial Director: Bonnie Dobkin
Editor and Curriculum Adviser: Suzanne Barchers
Program Manager: Gayatri Singh
Creative Director: Simmi Sikka
Project Manager: Santosh Vasudevan
Designer: Ritu Chopra
Picture Researcher: Judy Brown

Picture Credits
t–top b–bottom c–center l–left r–right

Cover: Imagesource/Photolibrary.

Back Cover: Sharif El-Hamalawi/Istockphoto.

Title page: Morgan Lane Photography/Istockphoto.

Insides: Orangeline/123F, Iofoto. 123RF: 3, Iofoto/123RF: 4, Masterfile: 5, Morgan Lane Photography/Istockphoto: 6, Imagesource/Photolibrary: 7, Anna Chelnokova/Istockphoto: 8, Mike Timberlake: 9, Zeljana Dubrovic/Istockphoto: 10t, Yuriy Kulyk/Shutterstock: 10b, Jerome Scholler/Shutterstock: 11l, Thomas Perkins/123RF: 11r, David Parsons/Istockphoto: 12t, Vladimir Kondrachov/Istockphoto: 12b, Jeremy Richards/Shutterstock: 13t, Doug Demarest/Photolibrary: 13b, Penelope Berger/Dreamstime: 14, Orange Line Media/Dreamstime: 15t, Rebecca Ellis/Istockphoto: 15bl, cfarmer/Dreamstime: 15br, Asia Images Group/Photolibrary: 16, Rmarmion/Fotolia: 17, Jon Feingersh/Photolibrary: 18, Octave Alex/Fotolia: 19, Sharif El-Hamalawi/Istockphoto: 20, Sema/Fotolia: 21, Istockphoto: 22, Elenathewise/Fotolia: 23, Dellison/Shutterstock: 24.

Teaching Strategies, Inc.
P.O. Box 42243
Washington, DC 20015
www.TeachingStrategies.com

ISBN: 978-1-60617-126-4

Library of Congress Cataloging-in-Publication Data
Stamper, Judith Bauer.
  A tree is for-- / Judith Bauer Stamper.
    p. cm.
  ISBN 978-1-60617-126-4
  1. Trees--Utilization--Juvenile literature. I. Title.
SD376.S73 2010
634.9'8--dc22
                              2009036424

CPSIA tracking label information:
RR Donnelley, Shenzhen, China
Date of Production: February 2011
Cohort: Batch 2

Printed and bound in China

| 2 3 4 5 6 7 8 9 10 | 15 14 13 12 11 |
|---|---|
| Printing | Year Printed |

What are trees for?
They're for giving us a cool spot to have a picnic.
Trees are for shade . . . and much, much more!

# A tree is for... having fun.

My swing hangs from a tree in my backyard.
When my dad pushes me, I fly high into the sky.

We climb up to play in our secret treehouse. A treehouse can be a pirate ship, a clubhouse, or even a spaceship.

Our family goes camping in the deep, dark woods.
At night, we tell spooky stories around the campfire.

Trees are great when you're playing hide and seek.
Don't peek before you're done counting!

# A tree is for... delicious food.

Apples, oranges, bananas, and pears all grow on trees. Have you ever picked a snack off a fruit tree?

Maple syrup comes from a tree, too. Just catch
the sap in a bucket to make sugar maple treats.

Look out below!
Nuts fall to the ground
under hickory, pecan, and
walnut trees. Squirrels like
nuts, too, so hurry to pick
the nuts you want!

Did you know that chocolate comes from a tree? The beans of the cacao tree are used to make frosting for this delicious cupcake.

# A tree is for... building houses.

All over the world, people live in houses made from trees.

This house in Peru sits on a riverbank. Wooden stilts keep the house high and dry.

Some people in Kenya built this roundhouse out of sticks. Its thatched roof looks like a hat.

This houseboat is made of bamboo. It floats through the backwaters of southern India.

This cabin is made from logs, cut from big branches and small tree trunks. Long ago, many Americans grew up in log cabins, including Abraham Lincoln!

People still use trees to build new houses.

At a lumber mill, people cut tree logs into wooden boards of different lengths and widths.

Carpenters nail the boards together to put up the house's frame. Next, they add a roof and walls.

They finish off the house with wooden floors and wooden doors.

When the house is done, a family moves into their new home.

15

# A tree is for... making all kinds of things.

This guitar is made from a soft wood.
It vibrates with music that makes you tap your feet.

This baseball bat is made from a hard
wood that's so strong it can hit a home run.

Wooden canoes are lightweight and easy to paddle.

Did you know that rubber comes from trees?
The tires on this bike came from the sap of a rubber tree.

Pick up your pencil and take a look.
It's made from a tree, too.

Even paper is made from trees. Paper factories
turn wood into pulp and press it into paper.
This book started out as a tree!

# A tree is for... making our planet a better place to live.

Trees clean our air when their leaves make food. The leaves take carbon dioxide out of the air and put oxygen back in.

Trees help the environment in many more ways. Their big, leafy branches keep houses cool on hot days. Their long, strong roots hold soil in place.

Best of all, trees make our planet beautiful.
What would our world be without trees?